11+ Maths

Year 5-7

Testpack B

(Arithmetic & Numerical Reasoning)

Practice Paper 9

Please read the following before you start the Practice Paper:

1. Do not begin the Practice Paper until you are told to do so.

2. The Practice Paper contains 50 questions and you have 45 minutes to complete it.

3. If you are doing the Practice Paper as a standard test, write your answers clearly in pencil. If you want to change an answer, put a single line through the wrong answer and write the correct answer clearly.

   If you are doing the Practice Paper as a multiple-choice test, draw a clear line through your chosen box in pencil. If you want to change an answer, rub it out and mark the correct box clearly. **Do not write on or mark the answer sheet in any way other than that which has been specified.**

4. There are 2 sections to this paper.

5. Each section includes an example showing you how to answer the questions. You may refer to these examples at any time as you work through the section.

6. Answer as many questions as you can; for some questions you will be given a range of options. If you get stuck on one of these questions, choose the answer that you think is most likely to be correct, then move on to the next question. If you get stuck on a question for which no options are given, leave it and move on to the next question. If you have time at the end of the section, go back and have another go at the questions you could not answer.

7. You may not use a calculator during this paper.

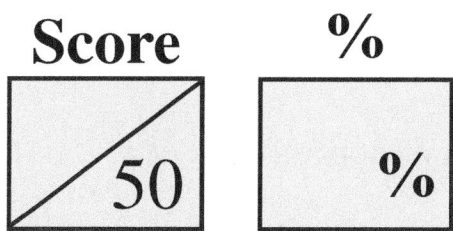

Score

%

/50

%

SECTION 1

EXAMPLE:

Read this example question. You may return to this example at any time as you work through this section.

Calculate 87 + 14.

A)   100   103   101   99   111

WAIT!

WAIT UNTIL YOU ARE TOLD TO GO ON

You have **15 minutes** to complete the **25 questions** in this section.

1) How many faces are there altogether on a cuboid and a triangular prism?   _____

2) What is the value of the 9 in 106.492?   _____

3) Fill in the gap:

$$\boxed{?} + 12 \times 3 = 108$$ _____

4) What percentage of £525 is £210?   _____

5) What is the lowest common denominator of $\frac{7}{12}$ and $\frac{3}{7}$? _____

6) Find the total volume of these three shapes:

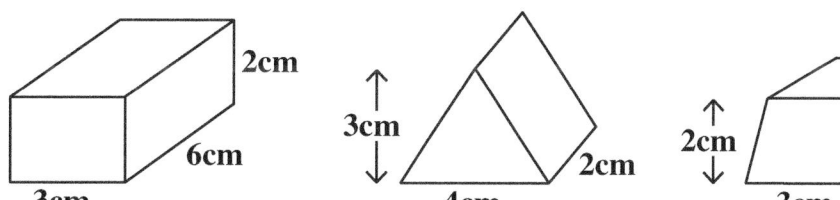

2cm

6cm

3cm

3cm

2cm

4cm

2cm

2cm

3cm

2cm

_____

7) Convert and calculate:

$21c\ell + 1.42\ell + 122m\ell$

Give the answer in litres. _____

8) $\frac{1}{5} \times (1\frac{1}{2} + 2\frac{2}{3})$ _____

9) Bradley's watch is 12 minutes fast. He checks his watch and it says 8.07am. What is the correct time? _____

10) What is the product of 2^3 and 7^2? _____

11) A survey of 62 people was conducted to find out how they travel to work. How many people take the bus?

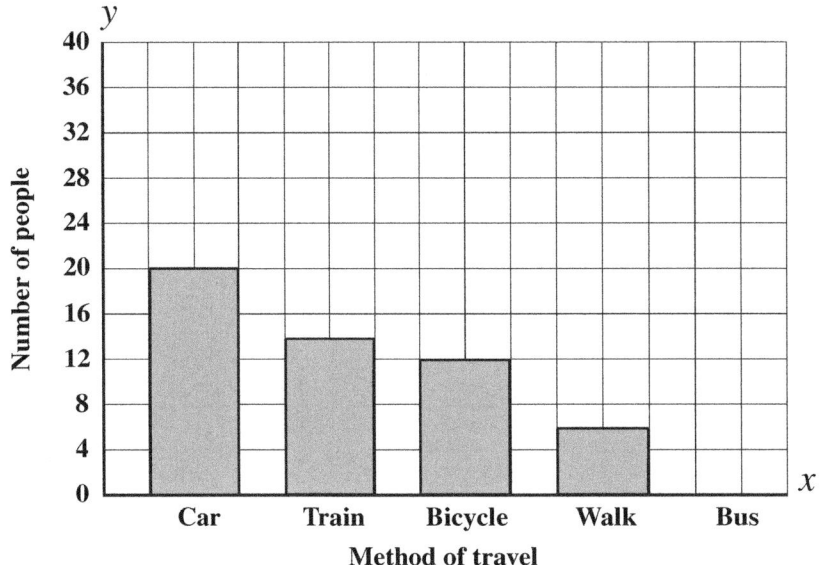

_____

12) Milk is sold in crates. Each crate contains sixteen 1ℓ bottles. A farmer has 1,000ℓ of milk to sell. How many crates will this fill? Give the answer in decimals.

_____

13) Rory is facing north-west. He turns 135° clockwise and then 90° clockwise again. Which direction is he now facing?

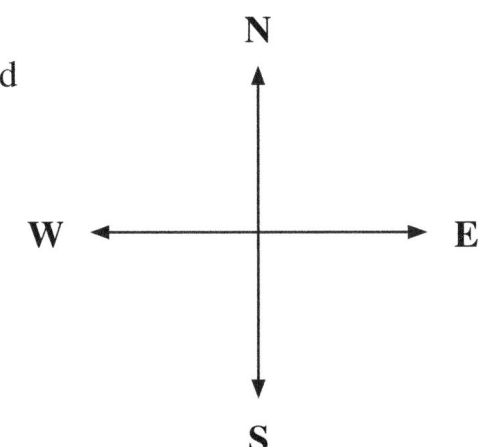

_____

14) Find the value of x:

$4x + 13 = 117$

_____

15) Serena has a piece of string that is 36cm long. She cuts the string into 3 lengths in the ratio 1 : 4 : 7.

What is the length of the longest piece of string?

_____

16) What is $\frac{5}{12}$ of £156? _____

17) Kiran is tiling her kitchen floor. The tiles she is using are 40cm long and 20cm wide. How many tiles will she need to cover the kitchen floor?

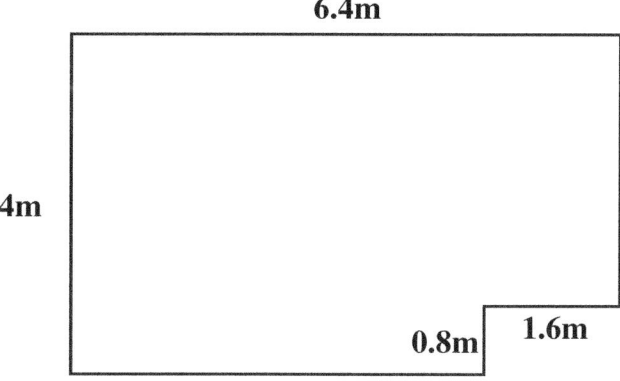

_____

18) There are 120 children in a school. A pie chart was made to show their different hair colours.

If 8 children have red hair, how many have brown hair?

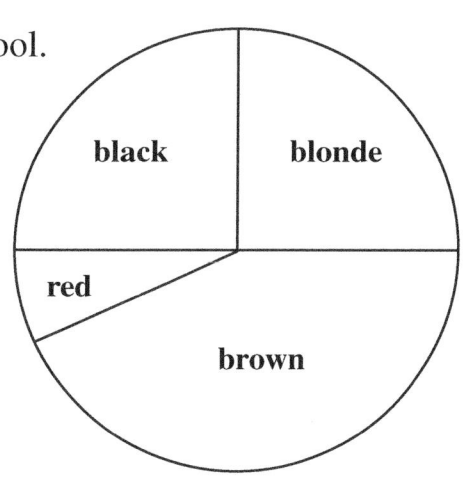

_____

19) Josh has 2ℓ of cola. He pours 120mℓ for himself and 130mℓ for Bhilhan. How much cola is left? _____mℓ

20) Cara has three dice. When she rolls the dice, what is the probability that she will throw three 4s? _____

21) Shannon wanted to record the rate of growth of her sunflower for a competition at school. In week 1 the sunflower was 21cm tall and in week 2 it was 26cm tall. If it continues to grow at the same rate as it did between weeks 1 and 2, how tall will Shannon's sunflower be at the end of the competition in week 6? _____

22) A triangular prism is 12cm long with a volume of 96cm^3. What is the cross-sectional area of the triangular prism? _____

23) A shape is reflected along the y axis of a graph.

What is the missing co-ordinate of the reflected shape?

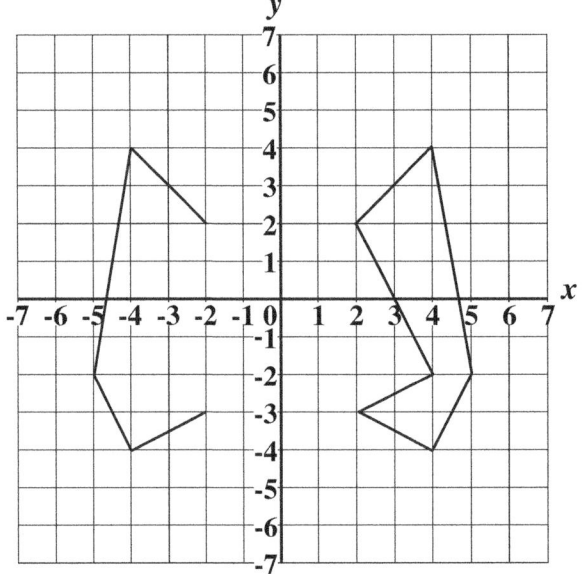

_____

24) Find the range of the numbers below:

12   18   27   8   32   21   _____

25) The average of three numbers is 6. When a fourth number is added the average becomes 9. What is the fourth number? _____

STOP!

YOU MAY CHECK YOUR ANSWERS IN THIS SECTION ONLY

BLANK PAGE

SECTION 2

WAIT!

WAIT UNTIL YOU ARE TOLD TO GO ON

You have **30 minutes** to complete the **25 questions** in this section.

Michael, Annie and Billy have stickers in the ratio 1 : 3 : 6.

1) If Annie has 63 stickers, how many does Billy have?   _____

2) How many more stickers does Annie have than Michael?   _____

3) How many stickers are there altogether?   _____

4) Billy gives 7 stickers to Annie and 14 stickers to Michael. What is the new ratio between Michael, Annie and Billy?   _____

5) Billy decides to share more stickers so that all three children have an equal amount. How many stickers does he need to give to Annie?   _____

Sandra's house is north of the church, east of the school, west of the shops and south of Mark's house.

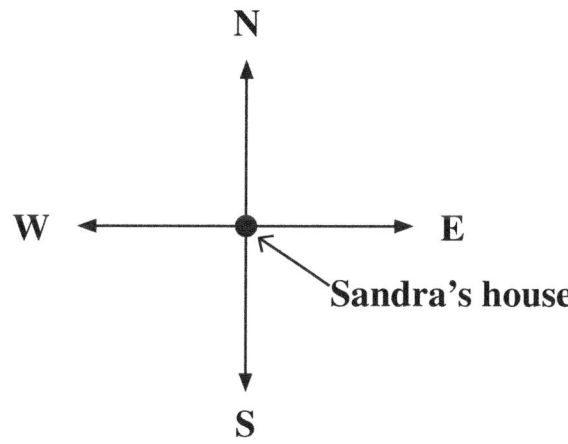

6) Mark's house is _____ of the church.   _____

7) The school is _____ of the church.   _____

8) Mark and Sandra agree to meet at the shops.
   Which direction does Mark have to walk from his house?   _____

9) Mark walks to Sandra's house in the morning so they can
   go to school together. In which direction do they walk to
   get to school?   _____

10) After school Mark and Sandra decide to go to the park, which is
    south of the school. In which direction do they have to walk to
    get back to Sandra's house afterwards?   _____

Adam has started training for a half marathon. He keeps a record of his running times for each training session. He runs 10 miles each time he trains.

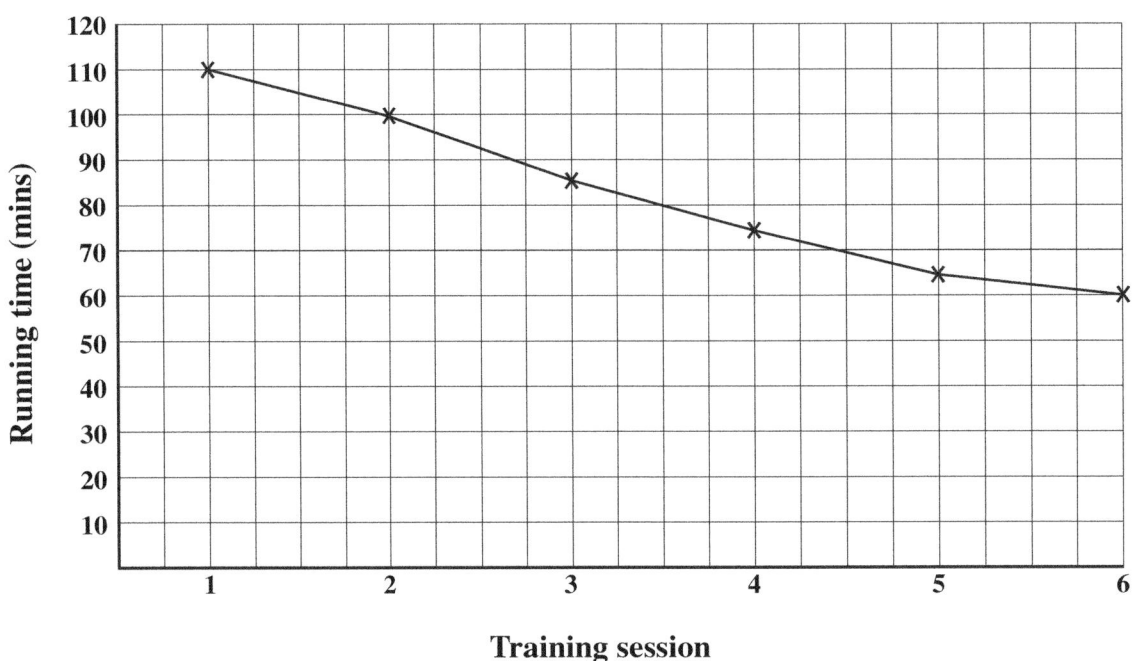

11) What was Adam's shortest running time? _____

12) By how many minutes has Adam improved his running time throughout his training? _____

13) What is Adam's average running time in minutes and seconds? _____

14) Adam ran 3 times a week during his training. His average running time for week one was 98min 20secs. What was the average time, in minutes and seconds, for week 2? _____

15) Adam wants to be able to run the 10 miles in 58mins. By how much does he need to improve his running time? _____

Danielle, Rose and Justine are stationery shopping. They see that folders have 20% off, pencil cases have 15% off, pens and pencils have 10% off and rubbers are 3 for the price of 2.

16) The original price for one folder was £8. How much will Danielle pay for three folders at the reduced price? _____

17) Justine needs a pencil case. She buys one reduced to £5.10. What was the original price? _____

18) Rose buys 3 pens and 2 pencils. The original price for pens was £2 and for pencils was £1. How much would she need to pay? _____

19) How much change will Rose get from a ten pound note? _____

20) How much more did Danielle spend than Justine? _____

Kim lives in Langley and regularly takes the train.

Here is the train timetable:

Stop	Train Timings			
Slough	07:32	08:02	08:33	09:07
Langley	07:38	08:08	08:39	09:13
Iver	07:49	08:19	08:50	09:24
West Drayton	08:00	08:30	09:01	09:35

21) How long does it take to get to Iver from Slough? _____

22) If Kim left Langley on the 08:08 train but the train was delayed by 6 minutes, what time would she get to West Drayton? _____

23) It takes Kim 12 minutes to walk from her house to Langley station and 5 minutes to buy a train ticket. What time does she need to leave home if she wants to catch the 08:08 train? _____

24) There are maintenance works on the train line between Langley and West Drayton which cause a 10 minute delay between each stop. If Kim catches the 09:13 train from Langley, what time will she get to West Drayton? _____

25) One day during the maintenance works, Kim needs to be in Iver by 9.00am. Which train does she need to catch from Langley? _____

STOP!

YOU MAY CHECK YOUR ANSWERS IN THIS SECTION ONLY

END OF PRACTICE PAPER

11+ Maths

Year 5-7

Testpack B

(Arithmetic & Numerical Reasoning)

Practice Paper 10

Please read the following before you start the Practice Paper:

1. Do not begin the Practice Paper until you are told to do so.

2. The Practice Paper contains 50 questions and you have 45 minutes to complete it.

3. If you are doing the Practice Paper as a standard test, write your answers clearly in pencil. If you want to change an answer, put a single line through the wrong answer and write the correct answer clearly.

    If you are doing the Practice Paper as a multiple-choice test, draw a clear line through your chosen box in pencil. If you want to change an answer, rub it out and mark the correct box clearly. **Do not write on or mark the answer sheet in any way other than that which has been specified.**

4. There are 2 sections to this paper.

5. Each section includes an example showing you how to answer the questions. You may refer to these examples at any time as you work through the section.

6. Answer as many questions as you can; for some questions you will be given a range of options. If you get stuck on one of these questions, choose the answer that you think is most likely to be correct, then move on to the next question. If you get stuck on a question for which no options are given, leave it and move on to the next question. If you have time at the end of the section, go back and have another go at the questions you could not answer.

7. You may not use a calculator during this paper.

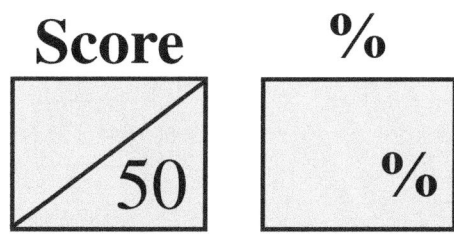

SECTION 1

EXAMPLE:

Read this example question. You may return to this example at any time as you work through this section.

Calculate 87 + 14.

A)   100   103   101   99   111
      ☐   ☐   ▬   ☐   ☐

WAIT!

WAIT UNTIL YOU ARE TOLD TO GO ON

You have **15 minutes** to complete the **25 questions** in this section.

1) How many vertices does a cube have?   _____

2) What is the mean of the following set of numbers?

    21   75   9   42   56   19   _____

3) Find the value of x:

    $6x + 5 = 12x - 7$ _____

4) The number machine below has an output of 398.

    Calculate the value of the input x.

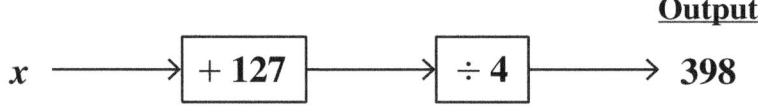

    Output
    $x \longrightarrow \boxed{+\,127} \longrightarrow \boxed{\div\,4} \longrightarrow 398$

                                                                          _____

5)

N

W ← → E

S

Benjamin is facing north-east. He turns 180° anticlockwise. He then turns 135° clockwise.

In what direction is Benjamin facing?

_____

6) What is the next number in the sequence?

3, 83, 123, 143, 153, ____

_____

7) John and James have 135 sweets. They share them in the ratio 3 : 2 with John receiving the larger share.

How many sweets does James have?

_____

8) What is the value of angle x?

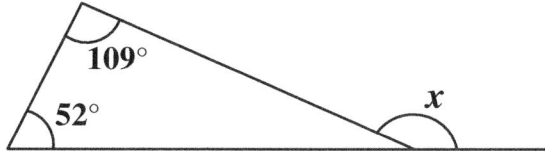

109°

52°

x

_____

9) Filip gets £3.46 pocket money when he helps his mum and dad. If he helps his mum and dad on the weekdays and also finds 8 pence, how much money does Filip have after one week?

_____

10) What is the probability of choosing a Jack, Queen or King of any suit from a deck of 52 playing cards? _____

11) What is 112% of 525? _____

12) Divide 17.6 by 1.8. Give the answer to 2 d.p. _____

13) 100 children were asked which pattern they liked best.

Calculate the missing value as a percentage.

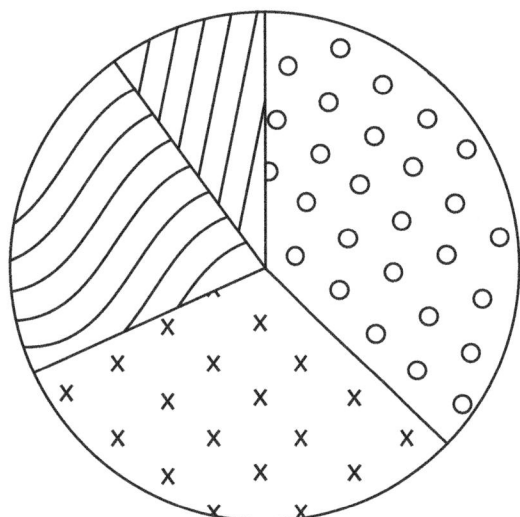

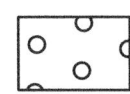 **40** children

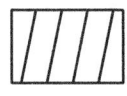 **5%** children

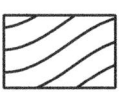 **?%** children

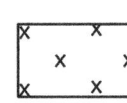 **30** children _____

14) What is the median of the following set of numbers?

128   79   9   156   127   105   51   196   205 _____

15) What is $\frac{17}{9} - \frac{15}{27}$ as a mixed number? _____

16) What is the difference in volume between shapes A and B?

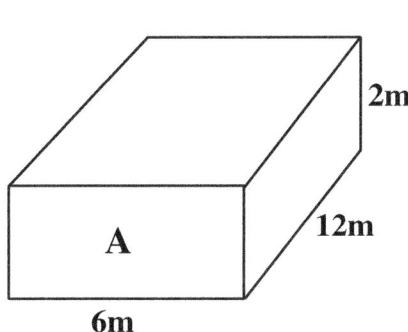 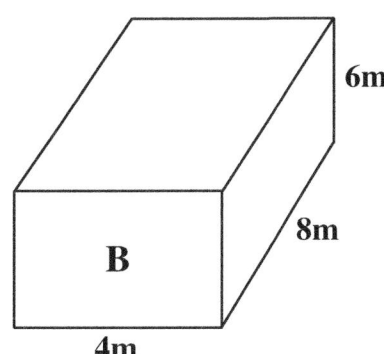

17) Loretta gets the 07:00 train from Salisbury to Basingstoke. She goes to the shops in Basingstoke for 22 minutes.

How many minutes must she wait for the next train from Basingstoke to Clapham Junction?

Stop	Time		
Salisbury	07:00	07:42	07:50
Andover	07:20	07:56	08:05
Basingstoke	07:25	08:06	08:15
Woking	07:50	08:26	08:37
Clapham Junction	08:12	08:32	08:52

18) John is 5 feet 6 inches tall. Jax is 4 feet 9 inches tall.

What is the difference of their heights in cm?

1 inch ≈ 2.5 centimetres

19) What is the value of $6^4 - 12^2$?

20) What is the 8th triangular number? _____

21) What is the sum of the first 6 triangular numbers? _____

22) How many faces does an octahedron have? _____

23)

This rectangle has a perimeter of 56cm.

$a + 2$

$a + 6$

What is the value of a? _____

24) Robyn's watch is 15 minutes slow. Her journey to school takes 10 minutes. At what time on her watch must she leave her house to arrive at school by 8.15am? _____

25) The sides of a ladder are _____ to the rungs of the ladder.

(parallel, perpendicular, complementary, opposite, intersecting) _____

STOP!

YOU MAY CHECK YOUR ANSWERS IN THIS SECTION ONLY

BLANK PAGE

SECTION 2

EXAMPLE:

Read this example question. You may return to this example at any time as you work through this section.

Amy and Declan both have Saturday jobs and get paid each week in the ratio 2 : 3. If Amy earns £24 per week, how much does Declan earn?

A)   £16   £48   £26   £12   £36
     ☐   ☐   ☐   ☐   ▬

WAIT!

WAIT UNTIL YOU ARE TOLD TO GO ON

You have **30 minutes** to complete the **25 questions** in this section.

A randomly selected group of students were asked if they liked rugby or football.

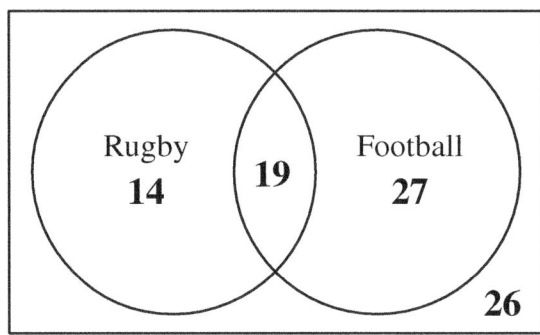

1) How many people were surveyed? _____

2) What fraction of students do not like football or rugby?
    (Answer in its lowest form.) _____

3) What percentage of students like both football and rugby?
    (Give the answer to 2 d.p.) _____

4) Of the students who only like football, $33\frac{1}{3}$% also like tennis.
    How many students only like football and no other sport? _____

5) The survey was carried out again with another group of students.
    98 out of the 368 students like football. The remainder all like
    rugby. What percentage of these students like rugby?
    (Give the answer to 2 d.p.) _____

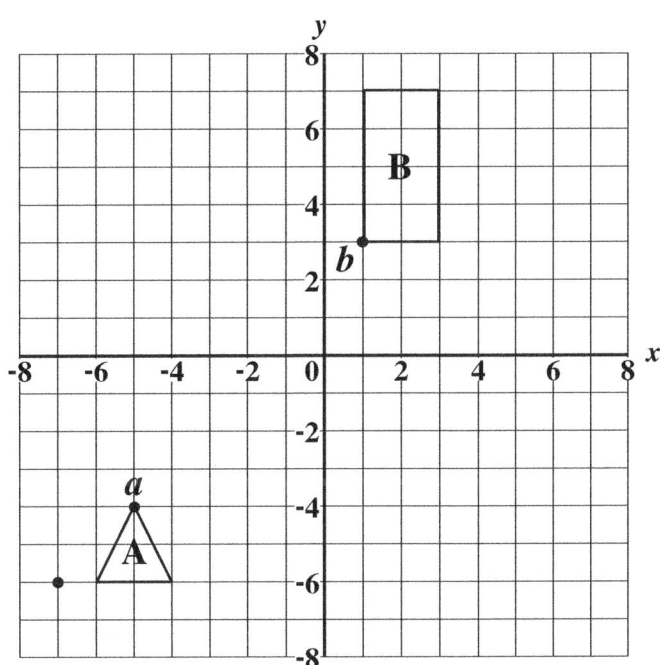

6) What will the co-ordinates of point *a* be if shape A is reflected in the *y* axis? _____

7) Rotate shape B anticlockwise by 270° about point *b*.
What are the new co-ordinates of the shape?

    A (3, 1) (3, 5) (1, 1) (1, 5)
    B (-3, 3) (5, 3) (-3, 5) (1, 5)
    C (1, 3) (5, 3) (1, 1) (5, 1)
    D (2, 3) (4, 3) (2, 1) (4, 1)
    E (1, 3) (-3, 1) (1, 1) (-3, 3) _____

8) Enlarge shape A by a scale factor of 2 from the point of enlargement (-7, -6).

What are the new co-ordinates of point *a*? _____

9) What will the co-ordinates of point *b* be if shape B is reflected in the *x* axis and then reflected in the *y* axis. _____

10) What transformation should be applied to point *a* so that the point is at the origin?

    A 4 right, 5 down
    B 3 right, 6 up
    C 5 right, 4 up
    D 4 left, 5 down
    E 6 right, 4 up _____

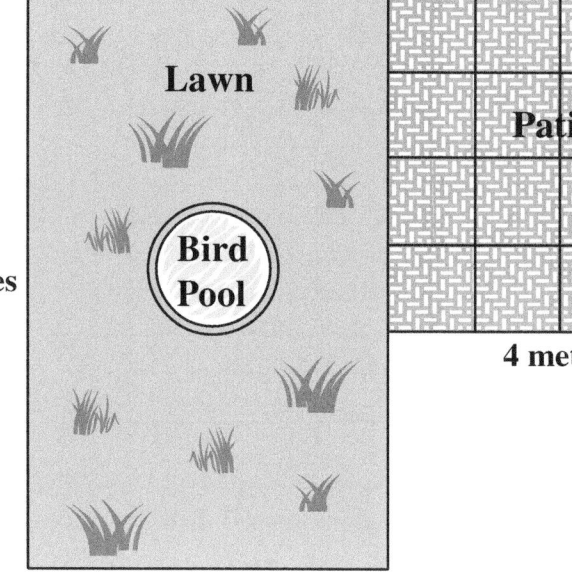

Garden
12 metres

Lawn

Patio

6 metres

11 metres

Bird Pool

4 metres

11) Calculate the perimeter of this garden. _____

12) Calculate the area of the patio. _____

13) The owner of this garden wants to replace the patio with a swimming pool which has a depth of 2.5 metres.

What will the volume of the swimming pool be? _____

14) The diameter of the bird pool is 140cm.

What is the radius of the bird pool in metres? _____

15) What is the circumference of the bird pool? ($\pi = 3.14$)

(Give the answer in metres to 2 d.p.) _____

Jameson received the following amounts of money over a 4-week period:

Week	1	2	3	4
Amount Received (£)	£525.00	£426.00	£27.52	£578.48

16) Calculate the mean amount of money received over this 4-week period. _____

17) What is the range of the 4-week period? _____

18) Jameson spends 20% of the money earned in this 4-week period on travel. How much does he spend on travel? _____

19) Of the money that remains, Jameson deposits 75% of it into a bank account. How much money does he have left after he deposits the 75%? _____

20) Jameson earns 5% interest on the money he has in his bank account at the end of every year. If he deposits the same amount of money into his bank account every 4 weeks for a year, what will be the total amount of money in his account? _____

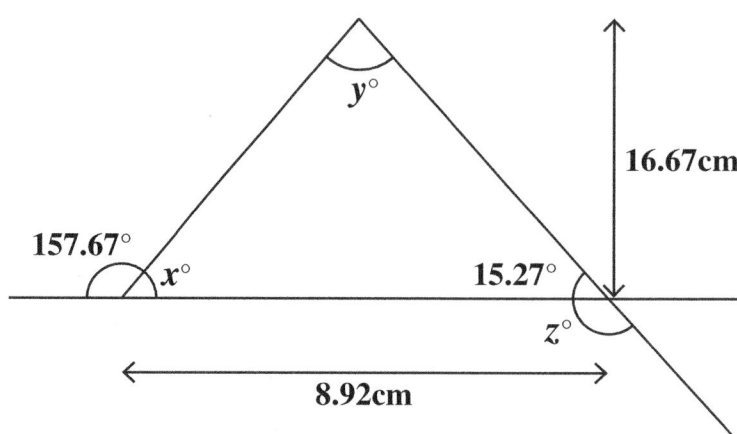

21) Calculate the size of angle *x*. _____

22) Calculate the size of angle *y*. _____

23) Calculate the size of angle *z*. _____

24) Calculate the area of the triangle. (Give the answer to 2 d.p.) _____

25) What type of angle is angle *x*?

(right angle, acute, obtuse, reflex, complementary) _____

STOP!

YOU MAY CHECK YOUR ANSWERS IN THIS SECTION ONLY

END OF PRACTICE PAPER

11+ Maths

Year 5-7

Testpack B

(Arithmetic & Numerical Reasoning)

Practice Paper 11

Please read the following before you start the Practice Paper:

1. Do not begin the Practice Paper until you are told to do so.

2. The Practice Paper contains 50 questions and you have 45 minutes to complete it.

3. If you are doing the Practice Paper as a standard test, write your answers clearly in pencil. If you want to change an answer, put a single line through the wrong answer and write the correct answer clearly.

   If you are doing the Practice Paper as a multiple-choice test, draw a clear line through your chosen box in pencil. If you want to change an answer, rub it out and mark the correct box clearly. **Do not write on or mark the answer sheet in any way other than that which has been specified.**

4. There are 2 sections to this paper.

5. Each section includes an example showing you how to answer the questions. You may refer to these examples at any time as you work through the section.

6. Answer as many questions as you can; for some questions you will be given a range of options. If you get stuck on one of these questions, choose the answer that you think is most likely to be correct, then move on to the next question. If you get stuck on a question for which no options are given, leave it and move on to the next question. If you have time at the end of the section, go back and have another go at the questions you could not answer.

7. You may not use a calculator during this paper.

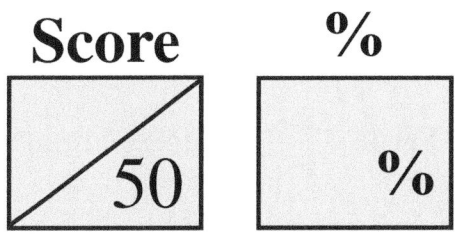

1

SECTION 1

EXAMPLE:

Read this example question. You may return to this example at any time as you work through this section.

Calculate $87 + 14$.

A) 100   103   101   99   111
     ▭   ▭   ▬   ▭   ▭

WAIT!

WAIT UNTIL YOU ARE TOLD TO GO ON

You have **15 minutes** to complete the **25 questions** in this section.

1) What is 28% of £54?   _____

2) What is the value of x?

$$4x + (3 \times 12) = 180$$

     _____

3) What is the area of this triangle?

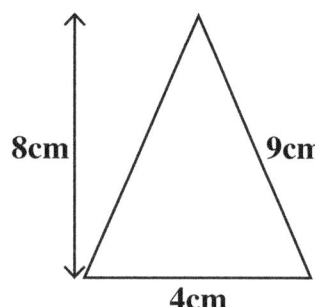

8cm   9cm

4cm   _____

4) Write $\dfrac{1596}{56}$ as a mixed number.   _____

5) What is the value of the 7 in 57,842.96? _____

6) If a coach leaves Peterborough for Beaconsfield at 9.47am and takes 2 hours and 24 minutes, at what time will it reach its destination? _____

7) Rose has 48 stickers. She shares them with Arnya and Serena in a ratio of 2 : 3 : 7 respectively. How many stickers does Rose have left once she has shared them out? _____

8) 489g + 2.49kg + 2,027g = ? _____kg

9) What is the area of this shape?

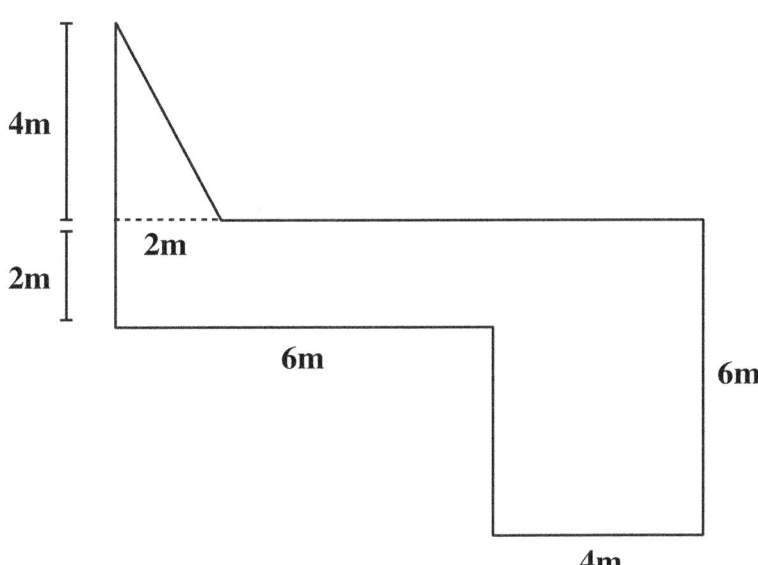

10) Claire spins an 8-sided fair spinner numbered 1-8.

What is the probability of landing on a prime number? _____

11) Hannah buys 12 cakes for £9.36 at a bakery. How many cakes could she buy with a £20 note? _____

12) Max does sit-ups everyday. For Monday to Friday his average is 67. On Saturday and Sunday his total is 148. What is Max's average for the week? _____

13)

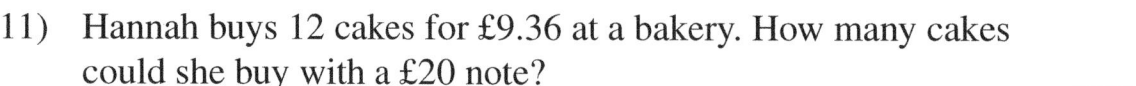

If Milos stands facing south-east and rotates clockwise by 270°, which direction will he be facing?

_____

14) If a number is halved, then multiplied by 3, then has a quarter of 16 added to it, the answer is 52. What is $\frac{3}{8}$ of that number? _____

15) How many sides does a decagon have? _____

16) Simran goes shopping in the sales. He buys a £50 jacket that has 70% off and an £85 pair of jeans that have 30% off.

How much did he spend in total? _____

17) Maria is plotting the corners of a rectangle on a graph. She has forgotten to draw the last corner.

What are the co-ordinates of the last corner?

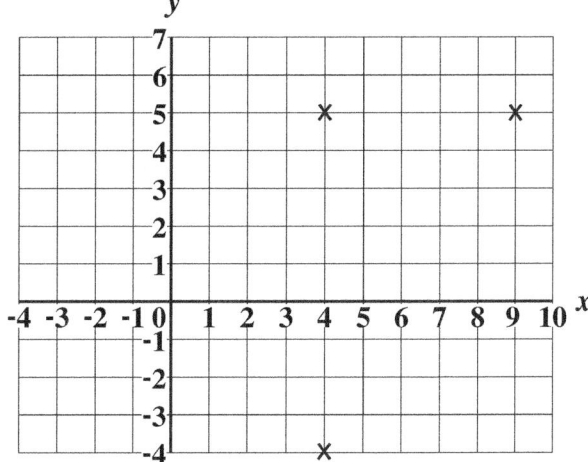

_____

18) What is the value of x in this sequence?

24,   28,   37, x,   78,   114 _____

19) What is 17,966 rounded to the nearest hundred? _____

20) Which of these letters has lines of symmetry and rotational symmetry?

N T H S B ___

21) Oliver has a random set of numbered cards. What is the mode?

4   12   3   7   9   14   8   12   3   7

17   7   10   10   12   7   4   8

7   9   3   7   14   8   7   _____

22) Maddie is making a patchwork quilt with a total area of 3.6m². Each square has a side of 12cm. How many squares does she need in total?   _____

23) If the 1st of April is a Wednesday, what day of the week is the 22nd of May?   _____

24) $\frac{9}{15} \div \frac{18}{40} = ?$ (Give the answer as a mixed number.)   _____

25) Michael has a kitten to whom he gives 125mℓ of milk twice a day. How many days would it take the kitten to drink a litre of milk?   _____

STOP!

YOU MAY CHECK YOUR ANSWERS IN THIS SECTION ONLY

BLANK PAGE

SECTION 2

EXAMPLE:

Read this example question. You may return to this example at any time as you work through this section.

Amy and Declan both have Saturday jobs and get paid each week in the ratio 2 : 3. If Amy earns £24 per week, how much does Declan earn?

A) £16   £48   £26   £12   £36
   ☐   ☐   ☐   ☐   ▬

WAIT!

WAIT UNTIL YOU ARE TOLD TO GO ON

You have **30 minutes** to complete the **25 questions** in this section.

George is about to start a new school so his parents give him £350 to get prepared.

1) George's school lunches cost £3.25 per day.

   How much is this per week?   _____

2) He has to buy a school uniform which costs him £70.00.

   What percentage is this of his £350?   _____

3) George then buys supplies for his lessons which cost him
   £87.65. After paying for his uniform and supplies, how
   much money does he have left?   _____

4) After buying his uniform and supplies he is ready for
   school. After four weeks of buying school lunches,
   how much money has he spent in total?   _____

5) How much money does he have left?   _____

Tom, Oli, Max and Nick are going skiing.
The holiday costs £780 per person.

6) Each lift pass costs £117. What percentage is that of the
total cost? _____

7) The accommodation costs $\frac{3}{8}$ of the total cost.

What is this equal to? _____

8) Oli and Max buy ski equipment before the holiday.
The equipment costs £210 each.

What is the new total cost for both Oli and Max to go together? _____

9) Nick is also taking his brother on a holiday later in the year.
This holiday costs him £520 per person for the flights plus
some additional costs per person:

Hotel = £210
Food = £175
Insurance = £25.50
Spending money = £135

What is the overall cost of this second holiday for Nick and
his brother? _____

10) Due to a flight delay, Nick and his brother have to stay on
holiday for an extra two nights. The airline company refunds
them £210 for the inconvenience. The hotel charges them
£25 each per additional night.

What is the new total cost of the holiday? _____

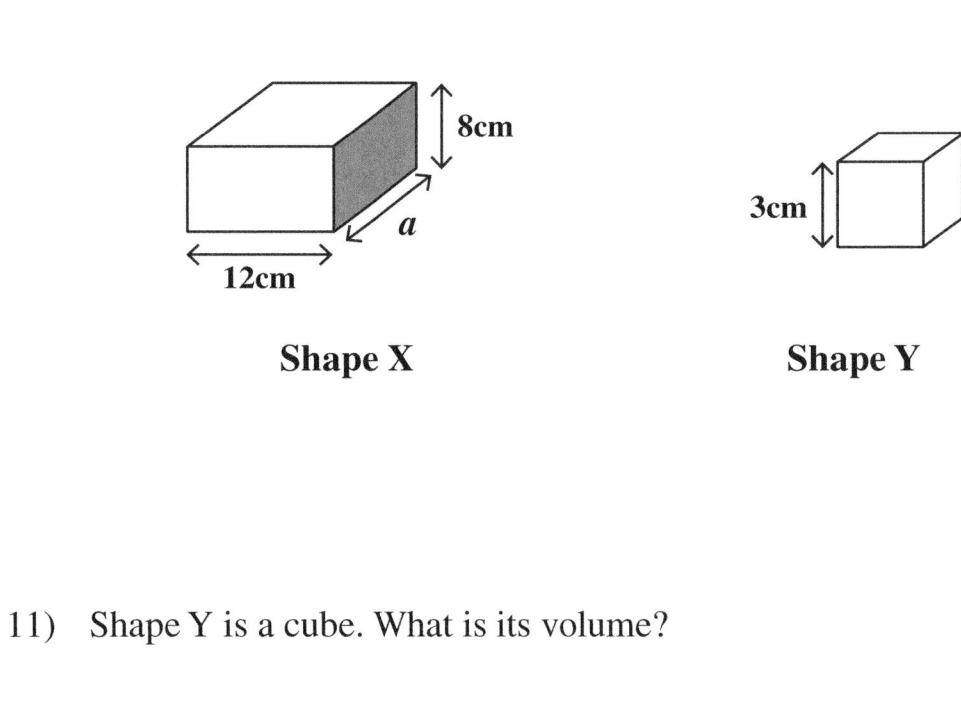

Shape X   **Shape Y**

11)   Shape Y is a cube. What is its volume?   _____

12)   The grey side of Shape X has an area of 32cm².

What is the depth (*a*)?   _____

13)   What is the volume of Shape X?   _____

14)   What is the surface area of Shape X?   _____

15)   What is the combined capacity of Shape X and Shape Y?   _____

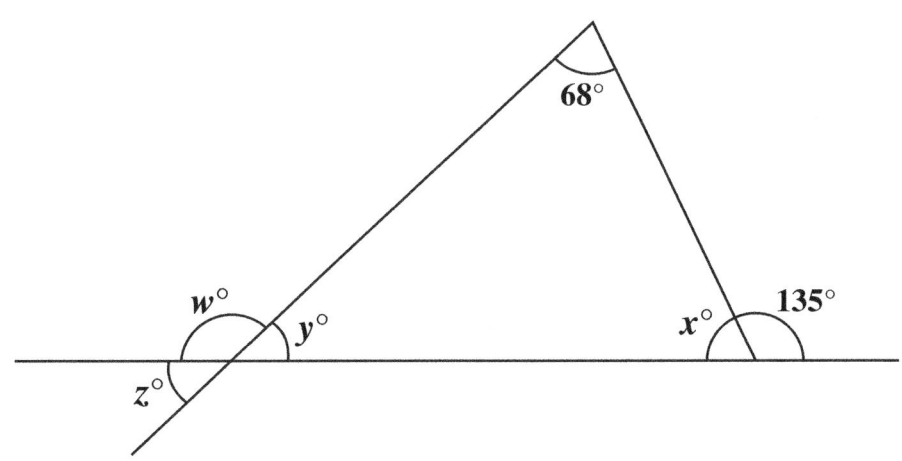

16) What is the size of angle *x*? _____

17) What is the size of angle *y*? _____

18) What is the size of angle *z*? _____

19) The width of this triangle is 7.2cm. The height is 6.5cm.

Find the area. _____

20) What is the size of angle *w*? _____

Nina has 10 numbered counters. They are shown below.

(4) (6) (13) (12) (2) (15) (16) (5) (3) (9)

21) What is the probability that Nina picks a square number? _____

22) What is the mean of the numbers on the counters? _____

23) What is the median of the numbers on the counters? _____

24) What is the percentage likelihood of Nina choosing an even number? _____

25) What is the probability of Nina picking a prime number? _____

STOP!

YOU MAY CHECK YOUR ANSWERS IN THIS SECTION ONLY

END OF PRACTICE PAPER

11+ Maths

Year 5-7

Testpack B

(Arithmetic & Numerical Reasoning)

Practice Paper 12

Please read the following before you start the Practice Paper:

1.   Do not begin the Practice Paper until you are told to do so.

2.   The Practice Paper contains 50 questions and you have 45 minutes to complete it.

3.   If you are doing the Practice Paper as a standard test, write your answers clearly in pencil. If you want to change an answer, put a single line through the wrong answer and write the correct answer clearly.

    If you are doing the Practice Paper as a multiple-choice test, draw a clear line through your chosen box in pencil. If you want to change an answer, rub it out and mark the correct box clearly. **Do not write on or mark the answer sheet in any way other than that which has been specified.**

4.   There are 2 sections to this paper.

5.   Each section includes an example showing you how to answer the questions. You may refer to these examples at any time as you work through the section.

6.   Answer as many questions as you can; for some questions you will be given a range of options. If you get stuck on one of these questions, choose the answer that you think is most likely to be correct, then move on to the next question. If you get stuck on a question for which no options are given, leave it and move on to the next question. If you have time at the end of the section, go back and have another go at the questions you could not answer.

7.   You may not use a calculator during this paper.

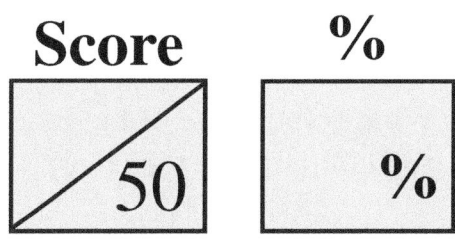

Score

%

/50

%

1

SECTION 1

EXAMPLE:

Read this example question. You may return to this example at any time as you work through this section.

Calculate 87 + 14.

A)   100   103   101   99   111

WAIT!

WAIT UNTIL YOU ARE TOLD TO GO ON

You have **15 minutes** to complete the **25 questions** in this section.

1)   What is the smallest positive prime number?   _____

2)   How many triangular numbers are there between 22 and 53?   _____

3)   1 inch roughly equals 2.5cm. How tall is Mr Moss in centimetres if he is 6 foot 2 inches tall?   _____

4)   What is the size of angle *f*?

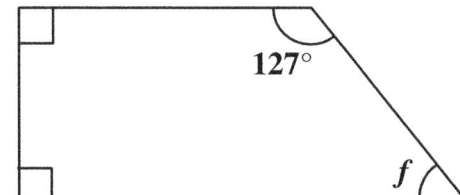

_____

5)   What is the name of the line that starts at the centre of a circle and continues to the edge?   _____

6) What is the quotient of 252 and 18? _____

7) A fountain pen costs Caitlin £0.45. She buys a number of fountain pens with a £5 note. If she received £0.95 change, how many pens did she buy? _____

8) What is the value of *x*?

$$\frac{5x}{2} + 8 = 2x + 17$$ _____

9) Nathan has a tortoise. He feeds it 400g of lettuce a day. If he buys a 2.65kg lettuce, for how many days can he feed his tortoise the full requirement before needing to buy another lettuce? _____

10)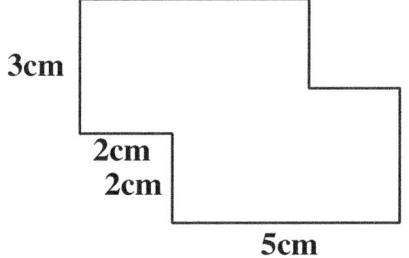

What is the perimeter of this shape? _____

11) A train is travelling at a constant speed. It is able to cover a distance of 220 miles in 330 minutes.

At what speed, in miles per hour, is the train moving? _____

12) Which of these shapes is not a regular polygon?

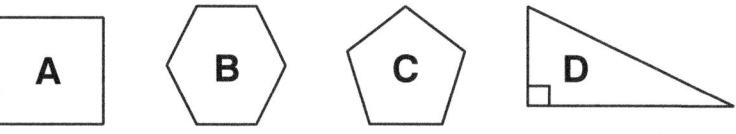

A   B   C   D   E   _____

13) In a sale customers get 15% off their purchases. If Zach buys a shirt for £15.30, what was the original price? _____

14) Riley is conducting an experiment. If she removes 0.62ℓ of water from a beaker containing $3,250m\ell$, what volume of water is left in the beaker in litres? _____

15) Fill in the missing number:

$8 + \underline{\quad} \times 12 = 80$ _____

16) The table below shows the time it takes five children to swim 50m:

Cori	**46.82s**
Keri	**46.802s**
Brad	**46.082s**
Alice	**46.208s**
Josh	**47.008s**

Who swam 50m in the second fastest time? _____

17) Solve the following calculation:

$\left(\dfrac{27}{30} + \dfrac{6}{15}\right) \times \dfrac{2}{3}$ _____

18) What is the lowest common multiple of 6, 8 and 9? _____

19) How many edges does a tetrahedron have? _____

20) What is the area of this triangle?

3.2mm

4.8mm

_____

21) Amber can write at a speed of 34 words per minute. If she needs to write a paper that is 6,800 words long, how long in hours and minutes will it take her to write? _____

22) What do the interior angles in a nonagon add up to? _____

23) Reynelle has a cube. She wants to colour it so that no two touching faces are the same colour.

What is the minimum amount of colours she needs to do this? _____

24) In a car park there are 700 spaces. 97 are filled by green cars, 86 are filled by blue cars, 184 are filled by silver cars and 153 are filled by black cars. How many spaces are vacant? _____

25) What is the value of the 6 in 3,764.28? _____

STOP!

YOU MAY CHECK YOUR ANSWERS IN THIS SECTION ONLY

SECTION 2

EXAMPLE:

Read this example question. You may return to this example at any time as you work through this section.

Amy and Declan both have Saturday jobs and get paid each week in the ratio 2 : 3. If Amy earns £24 per week, how much does Declan earn?

A) £16   £48   £26   £12   £36
    ▭   ▭   ▭   ▭   ▬

WAIT!

WAIT UNTIL YOU ARE TOLD TO GO ON

You have 30 minutes to complete the 25 questions in this section.

Raman has a bag of numbered balls. She asks her friend Orla to pick a ball from the bag.

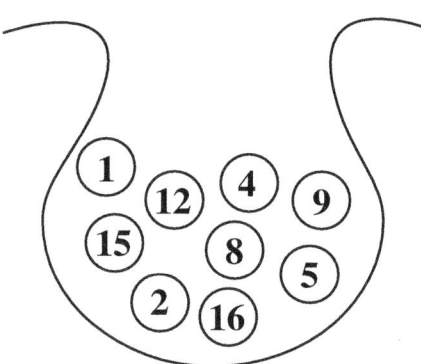

1) What is the probability that the ball is even?   _____

2) What fraction of the balls are either square or cube numbers?   _____

3) What is the mean of the balls' numbers?   _____

4) Raman decides to make this into a game. If a player picks out a multiple of 5, they win and receive a toy worth 65p. If the game costs 25p to play and 13 people play but only two win, how much profit has Raman made?   _____

5) What percentage of times should players win?
    (Round the answer to the nearest whole number.)   _____

Alex is learning about calories. He learns that 1 calorie is the equivalent of 4,200J or 4.2kJ (J = joules, the unit of energy).

6) How many kilojoules (kJ) are in a 250-calorie doughnut? _____

7) An apple is found to contain 268.8kJ.

How many calories are in this apple? _____

8) What is the difference in calories between a 300-calorie cake and a 701.4kJ cake? _____

9) Alex learns he needs 1,800 calories a day. If he has consumed 5287.8kJ for breakfast and lunch, how many calories must he consume for dinner? _____

10) Alex discovers he can burn off calories. He burns them off at a rate of 320 calories per hour of sport. Over a month he finds he has burnt off 5,120 calories.

How many hours of sport did he do that month? _____

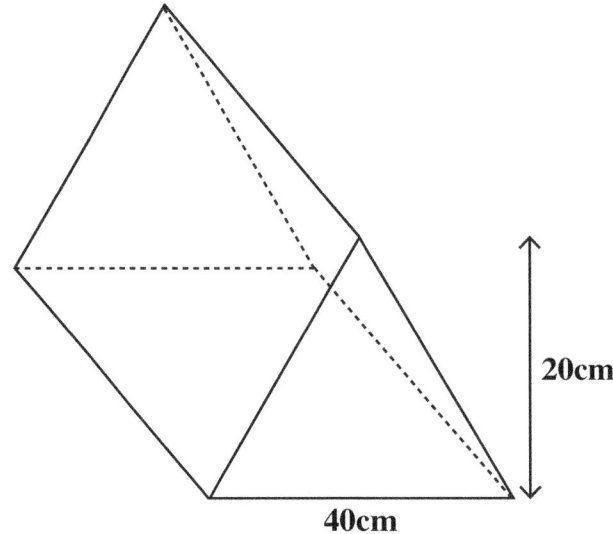

20cm

40cm

11)   What is the name of this shape?   _____

12)   What is the area of the cross-sectional shape?   _____

13)   If the shape is 1.2m long, what is the volume of the shape
      in cm^3?   _____

14)   The shape is cut in half to form two smaller versions of the shape.
      How many faces do these two shapes have in total?   _____

15)   Julia takes one of the new shapes and drops it in paint so that all
      the faces are covered. She then cuts it along the cross-section
      into 10 equal slices. How many faces will be covered in paint
      after cutting?   _____

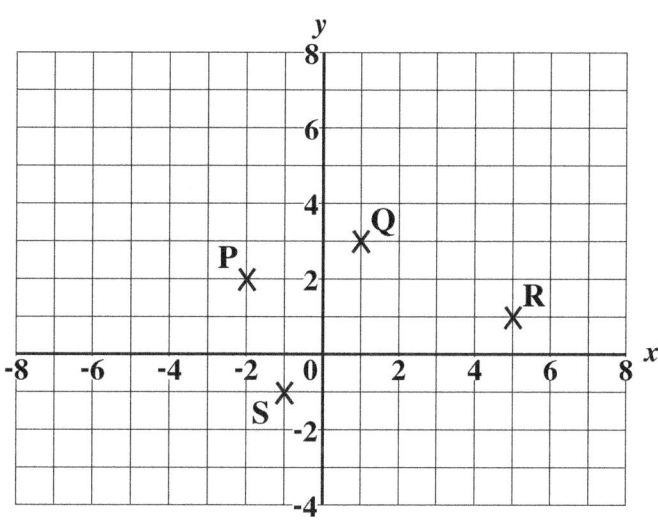

16)   What are the co-ordinates of P?   _____

17)   What are the co-ordinates of S?   _____

18)   The points PQRS are joined up.
      What shape do they make?   _____

19)   What translation is needed to move point R to point Q?   _____

20)   Point R is translated so that PQRS form a square.
      How is it translated?   _____

Rima has a recipe for apple pie. It is shown below:

<u>Apple Pie - for one pie which serves 6</u>

225g flour
125g sugar
3 large apples, sliced
6 medium eggs
50g butter

21)   In this recipe, what is the ratio of sugar to flour in its simplest form?   _____

22)   How much butter would be needed to make enough apple pies to serve 22 people?   _____

23)   Rima finds she can use 4 large eggs instead of 6 medium eggs. If the total weight of the eggs is the same, and a medium egg weighs 60g, how much does one large egg weigh?   _____

24)   Rima's dad finds a recipe that uses 20% less sugar and 20% less butter. What is the ratio of sugar to butter in his recipe?   _____

25)   If the new recipe uses 150g of flour, what fraction of the initial 225g is used?   _____

STOP!

YOU MAY CHECK YOUR ANSWERS IN THIS SECTION ONLY

END OF PRACTICE PAPER

Multiple-choice Answer Sheets
11+ Maths Year 5-7 Testpack B Practice Paper 9

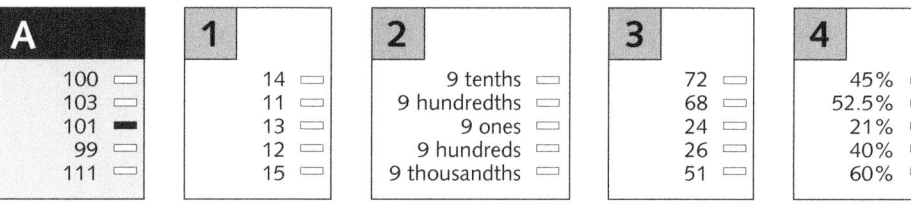

SECTION 1

A
- 100
- 103
- 101 ▬
- 99
- 111

1
- 14
- 11
- 13
- 12
- 15

2
- 9 tenths
- 9 hundredths
- 9 ones
- 9 hundreds
- 9 thousandths

3
- 72
- 68
- 24
- 26
- 51

4
- 45%
- 52.5%
- 21%
- 40%
- 60%

5
- 48
- 84
- 42
- 70
- 28

6
- 62cm³
- 36cm³
- 72cm³
- 60cm³
- 64cm³

7
- 3.642ℓ
- 1,752ℓ
- 1.752ℓ
- 4.74ℓ
- 17.52ℓ

8
- $^5/_6$
- $^7/_{10}$
- $^3/_5$
- $^2/_3$
- $^3/_4$

9
- 7.57am
- 8.15am
- 8.19am
- 7.53am
- 7.55am

10
- 294
- 336
- 392
- 84
- 384

11
- 12
- 10
- 14
- 8
- 11

12
- 62.5
- 6.25
- 62
- 625
- 60

13
- east
- south
- south-east
- north-east
- north

14
- 32
- 26
- 29
- 28
- 30

15
- 20cm
- 21cm
- 12cm
- 18cm
- 24cm

16
- £70
- £65
- £60
- £72
- £64

17
- 3,040
- 316
- 3,200
- 320
- 304

18
- 112
- 52
- 62
- 58
- 42

19
- 1,750mℓ
- 1.75mℓ
- 175mℓ
- 185mℓ
- 1.85mℓ

20
- $^3/_{216}$
- $^1/_{216}$
- $^3/_{18}$
- $^1/_6$
- $^3/_6$

21
- 45cm
- 41cm
- 46cm
- 51cm
- 50cm

22
- 9cm²
- 8cm²
- 8cm
- 1,152cm³
- 7cm²

23
- (-4, -1)
- (4, 2)
- (-4, -2)
- (-3, -2)
- (3, 2)

24
- 10
- 26
- 22
- 24
- 8

25
- 18
- 9
- 36
- 12
- 16

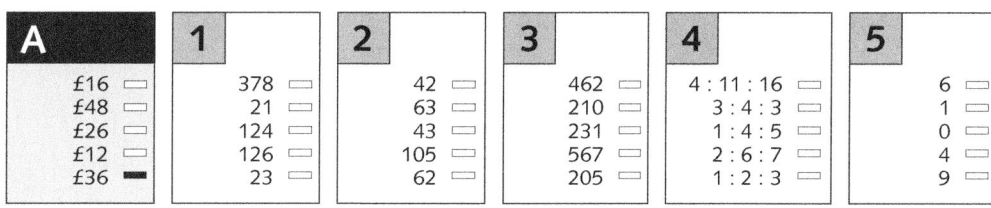

SECTION 2

A
- £16
- £48
- £26
- £12
- £36 ▬

1
- 378
- 21
- 124
- 126
- 23

2
- 42
- 63
- 43
- 105
- 62

3
- 462
- 210
- 231
- 567
- 205

4
- 4 : 11 : 16
- 3 : 4 : 3
- 1 : 4 : 5
- 2 : 6 : 7
- 1 : 2 : 3

5
- 6
- 1
- 0
- 4
- 9

6
- north
- south
- east
- west
- north-east

7
- west
- south-west
- north-west
- south-east
- south

8
- north-west
- south-east
- north-east
- south-west
- south

9
- west
- south-east
- east
- north-east
- south

10
- north-east
- south-east
- north-west
- south-west
- north

11
- 110mins
- 60mins
- 65mins
- 6mins
- 100mins

12
- 40mins
- 60mins
- 50mins
- 110mins
- 40mins

13
- 85mins 30secs
- 83mins 20secs
- 99mins
- 82mins 30secs
- 82mins

14
- 66mins 40secs
- 66mins 66secs
- 200mins
- 67mins 20secs
- 66mins

15
- 58mins
- 52mins
- 8mins
- 6mins
- 2mins

16
- £24.00
- £6.40
- £19.20
- £18.20
- £19.40

17
- £7.00
- £6.00
- £5.00
- £5.50
- £5.67

18
- £7.20
- £7.00
- £7.40
- £6.80
- £8.00

19
- £2.00
- £2.60
- £3.00
- £2.80
- £3.20

20
- £14.10
- £13.40
- £13.20
- £14.20
- £14.00

21
- 27 minutes
- 17 minutes
- 19 minutes
- 20 minutes
- 15 minutes

22
- 08:06
- 08:36
- 08:24
- 08:42
- 08:30

23
- 07:51
- 07:50
- 07:49
- 07:56
- 07:41

24
- 10:00
- 09:35
- 09:50
- 09:45
- 09:55

25
- 08:08
- 08:49
- 08:39
- 09:33
- 07:38

SECTION 1

A
- 100
- 103
- 101 ▬
- 99
- 111

1
- 12
- 4
- 8
- 16
- 6

2
- 36.50
- 36.25
- 36.75
- 36.00
- 37.00

3
- 5
- 3
- 6
- 2
- 4

4
- 1,465
- 1,433
- 1,460
- 1,687
- 1,719

5
- west
- east
- north-west
- south
- north

6
- 160
- 170
- 158
- 156
- 168

7
- 78
- 50
- 81
- 54
- 52

8
- 150°
- 21°
- 19°
- 161°
- 171°

9
- £17.28
- £17.56
- £17.38
- £17.24
- £17.30

10
- $\frac{12}{52}$
- $\frac{1}{13}$
- $\frac{8}{52}$
- $\frac{2}{13}$
- $\frac{3}{13}$

11
- 588
- 585.5
- 585.75
- 586.5
- 590

12
- 9.78
- 9.79
- 9.76
- 9.70
- 9.77

13
- 20%
- 12%
- 25%
- 15%
- 17%

14
- 196
- 127
- 105
- 128
- 79

15
- $1\frac{1}{3}$
- $2\frac{1}{3}$
- $3\frac{2}{3}$
- $\frac{5}{3}$
- $\frac{4}{3}$

16
- $50m^3$
- $42m^3$
- $58m^3$
- $46m^3$
- $48m^3$

17
- 20 minutes
- 19 minutes
- 21 minutes
- 3 minutes
- 18 minutes

18
- 22.7cm
- 22.6cm
- 22.8cm
- 22.5cm
- 22.75cm

19
- 1,512
- 108
- 432
- 215
- 1,152

20
- 28
- 30
- 49
- 36
- 45

21
- 29
- 21
- 48
- 52
- 56

22
- 6
- 9
- 3
- 8
- 7

23
- 10cm
- 12cm
- 6cm
- 8cm
- 11cm

24
- 7.55am
- 7.45am
- 7.50am
- 8.20am
- 8.00am

25
- parallel
- perpendicular
- complementary
- opposite
- intersecting

SECTION 2

A
- £16
- £48
- £26
- £12
- £36 ▬

1
- 82
- 86
- 67
- 75
- 91

2
- $\frac{13}{61}$
- $\frac{12}{20}$
- $\frac{18}{40}$
- $\frac{13}{43}$
- $\frac{7}{16}$

3
- 22.09%
- 23.07%
- 22.01%
- 22.2%
- 22.5%

4
- 9
- 27
- 3
- 15
- 18

5
- 74.28%
- 73.26%
- 73.58%
- 73.37%
- 73.31%

6
- (-5, -4)
- (-4, 5)
- (4, -5)
- (5, -4)
- (-5, 4)

7
- A
- B
- C
- D
- E

8
- (3, 1)
- (-2, -1)
- (-3, -2)
- (-7, -6)
- (-2, -3)

9
- (1, -3)
- (-1, -3)
- (-3, 1)
- (-2, -4)
- (1, 3)

10
- A
- B
- C
- D
- E

11
- 40m
- 45m
- 46m
- 50m
- 56m

12
- $24m^2$
- $48m^2$
- $74m^2$
- $40m^2$
- $72m^2$

13
- $50m^3$
- $60m^3$
- $40m^3$
- $48m^3$
- $55m^3$

14
- 7m
- 70m
- 0.7m
- 0.55m
- 70cm

15
- 6.10m
- 5.20m
- 4.65m
- 4.40m
- 5.70m

16
- £389.25
- £389.00
- £389.50
- £389.75
- £389.80

17
- £550.68
- £550.92
- £550.75
- £550.96
- £550.90

18
- £311.50
- £311.60
- £311.40
- £311.70
- £311.30

19
- £311.50
- £311.70
- £311.60
- £311.30
- £311.40

20
- £12,751.83
- £12,561.92
- £1,342.56
- £627.26
- £12,892.51

21
- 22.36°
- 22.39°
- 22.37°
- 22.33°
- 22.30°

22
- 143.8°
- 142.4°
- 147.9°
- 146.6°
- 142.5°

23
- 164.82°
- 164.75°
- 164.89°
- 164.77°
- 164.73°

24
- $74.26cm^2$
- $74.34cm^2$
- $74.36cm^2$
- $74.35cm^2$
- $74.92cm^2$

25
- right angle
- acute
- obtuse
- reflex
- complementary

SECTION 1

A
- 100
- 103
- 101 ▬
- 99
- 111

1
- £14.86
- £26
- £15.12
- £1.51
- £1.74

2
- 54
- 9
- 40
- 37
- 36

3
- 21cm²
- 36cm²
- 16cm²
- 18cm²
- 32cm²

4
- 28¹/₂
- 28²⁸/₅₆
- 27¹/₂
- 29¹/₂
- 57¹/₂

5
- 70 thousand
- 7 hundredths
- 7 hundreds
- 7 thousand
- 7 thousandths

6
- 12.11am
- 11.47am
- 12.07pm
- 12.15pm
- 12:11pm

7
- 2
- 8
- 12
- 28
- 6

8
- 5.006kg
- 50.06kg
- 500.6kg
- 50.16kg
- 5.016kg

9
- 60m²
- 40m²
- 44m²
- 30m²
- 36m²

10
- ³/₄
- ¹/₈
- ⁵/₈
- ¹/₂
- ³/₈

11
- 25
- 26
- 27
- 28
- 29

12
- 65
- 69
- 32
- 74
- 55

13
- south-west
- west
- north
- north-west
- north-east

14
- 18
- 20
- 12
- 32
- 15

15
- 8
- 15
- 20
- 10
- 12

16
- £74.50
- £60.50
- £94.50
- £50.50
- £35.00

17
- (9, -4)
- (9, 4)
- (-4, 9)
- (9, 3)
- (9, -3)

18
- 50
- 53
- 57
- 46
- 58

19
- 17,970
- 18,900
- 17,800
- 18,000
- 17,900

20
- N
- T
- H
- S
- B

21
- 10
- 9
- 14
- 8
- 7

22
- 250
- 25
- 2,500
- 2.5
- 30

23
- Monday
- Tuesday
- Thursday
- Friday
- Saturday

24
- 1¹/₁₈
- 1¹/₃
- 1¹/₂
- 1¹/₁₅
- 1³/₄₀

25
- 8
- 2
- 3
- 4
- 5

SECTION 2

A
- £16
- £48
- £26
- £12
- £36 ▬

1
- £22.75
- £19.50
- £16.75
- £15.00
- £16.25

2
- 28%
- 0.2%
- 35%
- 25%
- 20%

3
- £262.35
- £200.00
- £280.00
- £215.35
- £192.35

4
- £222.65
- £65.00
- £235.00
- £127.35
- £250.35

5
- £285.00
- £127.35
- £152.65
- £165.25
- £135.00

6
- 17%
- 19%
- 14%
- 15%
- 20%

7
- £97.50
- £292.50
- £210.40
- £307.00
- £260.00

8
- £1,980
- £420
- £1,770
- £2,000
- £1,560

9
- £1,065.50
- £1,585.50
- £2,131
- £2,000
- £2,130

10
- £2,131
- £1,475.5
- £2,021
- £955.50
- £2,020

11
- 9cm³
- 12cm³
- 27cm³
- 8cm³
- 36cm³

12
- 7.5cm
- 4cm
- 12cm
- 256cm
- 5cm

13
- 400cm³
- 384cm³
- 96cm³
- 94cm³
- 192cm³

14
- 384cm²
- 256cm²
- 352cm²
- 32cm²
- 64cm²

15
- 411cm³
- 357cm³
- 401cm³
- 375cm³
- 428cm³

16
- 56°
- 45°
- 135°
- 90°
- 112°

17
- 67°
- 135°
- 69°
- 59°
- 78°

18
- 113°
- 45°
- 90°
- 67°
- 82°

19
- 46.8cm²
- 27.4cm²
- 13.7cm²
- 23.4cm²
- 25.5cm²

20
- 67°
- 113°
- 82°
- 145°
- 180°

21
- ³/₁₀
- ²/₁₀
- ¹/₄
- ¹/₁₀
- ¹/₂

22
- 14
- 9
- 8.5
- 7.5
- 8.7

23
- 6
- 9
- 7.5
- 7
- 8.5

24
- 50%
- 25%
- 60%
- 20%
- 10%

25
- ²/₅
- ¹/₁₀
- ⁷/₁₀
- ⁴/₅
- ³/₁₀

SECTION 1

A
- 100
- 103
- 101 ■
- 99
- 111

1
- 1
- 2
- 3
- 4
- 5

2
- 1
- 2
- 3
- 4
- 5

3
- 1.55cm
- 195cm
- 1.92cm
- 185cm
- 163cm

4
- 53°
- 3°
- 233°
- 223°
- 47°

5
- radius
- circumference
- diameter
- chord
- tangent

6
- 16
- 18
- 22
- 12
- 14

7
- 6
- 7
- 8
- 9
- 10

8
- 16
- 18
- 22
- 24
- 26

9
- 8
- 5
- 7
- 9
- 6

10
- 12cm
- 28cm
- 32cm
- 24cm
- 18cm

11
- 70mph
- 40mph
- 90mph
- 60mph
- 50mph

12
- A
- B
- C
- D
- E

13
- £13.05
- £15.50
- £16.00
- £18.00
- £2.30

14
- 3.188ℓ
- 2.62ℓ
- 2.95ℓ
- 2.63ℓ
- 3.87ℓ

15
- 2
- 3
- 4
- 5
- 6

16
- Cori
- Keri
- Brad
- Alice
- Josh

17
- $^7/_6$
- $^6/_{10}$
- $^{13}/_{15}$
- $^8/_5$
- $^4/_5$

18
- 24
- 36
- 48
- 64
- 72

19
- 4
- 5
- 6
- 7
- 8

20
- 8mm²
- 7.68mm²
- 6.42mm²
- 15.36mm²
- 10.18mm²

21
- 3hrs 20mins
- 3hrs 30mins
- 3hrs 40mins
- 3hrs 50mins
- 4hrs

22
- 720°
- 900°
- 1,080°
- 1,260°
- 1,440°

23
- 2
- 3
- 4
- 5
- 6

24
- 190
- 140
- 160
- 180
- 150

25
- 6 hundreds
- 6 tenths
- 6 hundredths
- 6 thousandths
- 6 tens

SECTION 2

A
- £16
- £48
- £26
- £12
- £36 ■

1
- $^2/_9$
- $^1/_3$
- $^5/_9$
- $^4/_9$
- $^2/_3$

2
- $^5/_9$
- $^4/_9$
- $^1/_3$
- $^2/_9$
- $^1/_9$

3
- 3
- 4
- 5
- 8
- 7

4
- £2.95
- £1.95
- £2.15
- £2.25
- £2.35

5
- 56%
- 78%
- 11%
- 33%
- 22%

6
- 1,125kJ
- 1,100kJ
- 1,075kJ
- 1,050kJ
- 1,025kJ

7
- 64 calories
- 62 calories
- 60 calories
- 58 calories
- 56 calories

8
- 143 calories
- 138 calories
- 133 calories
- 128 calories
- 123 calories

9
- 571 calories
- 561 calories
- 551 calories
- 541 calories
- 531 calories

10
- 12 hours
- 14 hours
- 16 hours
- 18 hours
- 20 hours

11
- cuboid
- triangular prism
- cylinder
- cube
- tetrahedron

12
- 400cm²
- 600cm²
- 700cm²
- 800cm²
- 500cm²

13
- 32,000cm³
- 40,000cm³
- 48,000cm³
- 44,000cm³
- 36,000cm³

14
- 5
- 10
- 8
- 7
- 12

15
- 24
- 30
- 26
- 28
- 32

16
- (-2, -2)
- (-2, 2)
- (-1, -1)
- (-3, 2)
- (2, -2)

17
- (2, -2)
- (-1, -1)
- (1, 5)
- (-2, 2)
- (5, 1)

18
- square
- parallelogram
- trapezium
- rectangle
- rhombus

19
- 4 right, 2 up
- 4 right, 2 down
- 3 left, 2 up
- 3 right, 2 up
- 4 left, 2 up

20
- 3 left, 1 down
- 4 left, 2 down
- 4 left, 1 down
- 3 left, 2 down
- 5 left, 2 down

21
- 25 : 45
- 15 : 27
- 6 : 10
- 2 : 3
- 5 : 9

22
- 50g
- 100g
- 150g
- 200g
- 250g

23
- 45g
- 70g
- 90g
- 110g
- 135g

24
- 4 : 6
- 5 : 2
- 2 : 5
- 10 : 4
- 3 : 2

25
- $^2/_3$
- $^1/_4$
- $^1/_2$
- $^3/_4$
- $^1/_3$

11+ Maths

Year 5-7

Testpack B
(Arithmetic & Numerical Reasoning)

Practice Papers 9-12

Answers and guidance notes for parents

These practice papers can be completed as standard or multiple-choice tests.

Multiple-choice Tests

Your child should mark their answers on the multiple-choice answer sheets. It is important for them to treat it like the real thing and record an answer in the appropriate box by drawing a clear line through their chosen box with a pencil. Clarity is important as the actual test would be marked by a computer. Mistakes should be carefully rubbed out and not crossed out since this would not be correctly recorded by the computer.

Standard Tests

Ask your child to fill in the answers in the spaces as instructed in each section. Mistakes should be crossed through with a single line and the correct answer written clearly.

Marking and Feedback

The answers are provided in this booklet. Only these answers are allowed. One mark should be given for each correct answer. Do not deduct marks for wrong answers. Do not allow half marks or 'benefit of the doubt', as this might mask a child's need for extra help in the topic and does not replicate the real exam conditions. Always try to be positive and encouraging. Talk through any mistakes with your child and work out together how to arrive at the correct answer.

Timing

The practice papers are split into individually timed sections. Each section contains an example question which is not timed. However, there is also the option to complete each paper in one sitting of 45 minutes, without timing each section.

Score	%	Score	%	Score	%	Score	%	Score	%
1	2%	11	22%	21	42%	31	62%	41	82%
2	4%	12	24%	22	44%	32	64%	42	84%
3	6%	13	26%	23	46%	33	66%	43	86%
4	8%	14	28%	24	48%	34	68%	44	88%
5	10%	15	30%	25	50%	35	70%	45	90%
6	12%	16	32%	26	52%	36	72%	46	92%
7	14%	17	34%	27	54%	37	74%	47	94%
8	16%	18	36%	28	56%	38	76%	48	96%
9	18%	19	38%	29	58%	39	78%	49	98%
10	20%	20	40%	30	60%	40	80%	50	100%

Answers

Practice Paper 9

Section 1
1) 11
2) 9-hundredths or 0.09
3) 72
4) 40%
5) 84
6) 60cm³
7) 1.752ℓ
8) ⁵/₆
9) 7.55am
10) 392
11) 10
12) 62.5
13) south
14) 26
15) 21cm
16) £65
17) 304
18) 52
19) 1,750mℓ
20) ¹/₂₁₆
21) 46cm
22) 8cm²
23) (-4, -2)
24) 24
25) 18

Section 2
1) 126
2) 42
3) 210
4) 1 : 2 : 3
5) 0
6) north
7) north-west
8) south-east
9) west
10) north-east
11) 60mins
12) 50mins
13) 82mins 30secs
14) 66mins 40secs
15) 2mins
16) £19.20
17) £6.00
18) £7.20
19) £2.80
20) £14.10
21) 17 minutes
22) 08:36
23) 07:51
24) 09:55
25) 08:39

Practice Paper 10

Section 1
1) 8
2) 37
3) 2
4) 1,465
5) north
6) 158
7) 54
8) 161°
9) £17.38
10) ³/₁₃
11) 588
12) 9.78
13) 25%
14) 127
15) 1¹/₃
16) 48m³
17) 19 minutes
18) 22.5cm
19) 1,152
20) 36
21) 56
22) 8
23) 10cm
24) 7.50am
25) perpendicular

Section 2
1) 86
2) ¹³/₄₃
3) 22.09%
4) 18
5) 73.37%
6) (5, -4)
7) C
8) (-3, -2)
9) (-1, -3)
10) C
11) 46m
12) 24m²
13) 60m³
14) 0.7m
15) 4.40m
16) £389.25
17) £550.96
18) £311.40
19) £311.40
20) £12,751.83
21) 22.33°
22) 142.4°
23) 164.73°
24) 74.35cm²
25) acute

Answers

Practice Paper 11

Section 1
1) £15.12
2) 36
3) 16cm^2
4) 28$^1/_2$
5) 7 thousand or 7,000
6) 12.11pm
7) 8
8) 5.006kg
9) 40m^2
10) $^1/_2$
11) 25
12) 69
13) north-east
14) 12
15) 10
16) £74.50
17) (9, -4)
18) 53
19) 18,000
20) H
21) 7
22) 250
23) Friday
24) 1$^1/_3$
25) 4

Section 2
1) £16.25
2) 20%
3) £192.35
4) £222.65
5) £127.35
6) 15%
7) £292.50
8) £1,980
9) £2,131
10) £2,021
11) 27cm^3
12) 4cm
13) 384cm^3
14) 352cm^2
15) 411cm^3
16) 45°
17) 67°
18) 67°
19) 23.4cm^2
20) 113°
21) $^3/_{10}$
22) 8.5
23) 7.5
24) 50%
25) $^2/_5$

Practice Paper 12

Section 1
1) 2
2) 3
3) 185cm
4) 53°
5) radius
6) 14
7) 9
8) 18
9) 6
10) 24cm
11) 40mph
12) D
13) £18.00
14) 2.63ℓ
15) 6
16) Alice
17) $^{13}/_{15}$
18) 72
19) 6
20) 7.68mm^2
21) 3hrs 20mins
22) 1,260°
23) 3
24) 180
25) 6 tens

Section 2
1) $^5/_9$
2) $^5/_9$
3) 8
4) £1.95
5) 22%
6) 1,050kJ
7) 64 calories
8) 133 calories
9) 541 calories
10) 16 hours
11) triangular prism
12) 400cm^2
13) 48,000cm^3
14) 10
15) 32
16) (-2, 2)
17) (-1, -1)
18) trapezium
19) 4 left, 2 up
20) 3 left, 1 down
21) 5 : 9
22) 200g
23) 90g
24) 5 : 2
25) $^2/_3$

PROGRESS CHARTS

Paper	Total Score	Percentage
Practice Paper 9	/ 50	%
Practice Paper 10	/ 50	%
Practice Paper 11	/ 50	%
Practice Paper 12	/ 50	%

Overall Percentage | % | For the average add up % and divide by 4